D1518868

New York

# KNICKS

BY JIM GIGLIOTTI

Published by The Child's World®
1980 Lookout Drive • Mankato, MN 56003-1705
800-599-READ • www.childsworld.com

ISBN 9781503824478
LCCN 2018964289

Printed in the United States of America
PA02416

## ABOUT THE AUTHOR

Jim Gigliotti has worked for the University
of Southern California's athletic department,
the Los Angeles Dodgers, and the National
Football League. He is now an author who
has written more than 100 books, mostly
for young readers, on a variety of topics.

# TABLE OF

# CONTENTS

# GO, KNICKS!

**T**he Knicks have had many great players. They have had many great moments. And they have had many good, but usually not great, teams. That is the good news and the bad news. The Knicks have made the playoffs 42 times in their 73 seasons. They have only won two titles, though. Their last was in 1973. Knicks fans hope that **drought** ends soon.

The Knicks young guard Emmanuel Mudiay shows New York toughness against the 76ers.

Noah Vonleh scores for the Knicks against the Atlanta Hawks, an Eastern Conference opponent.

# WHO ARE THE KNICKS?

The Knicks play in the Atlantic Division. That division is part of the NBA's Eastern Conference. The other teams in the Atlantic Division are the Boston Celtics, the Brooklyn Nets, the Philadelphia 76ers, and the Toronto Raptors. The Knicks have played in the Atlantic since the division began in 1971. They won the first Atlantic Division title that season.

# WHERE THEY CAME FROM

The Knicks began playing in the Basketball Association of America (BAA) in 1947. The BAA and another league formed the NBA in 1949. The Knicks have always played in New York. The team's full name is Knickerbockers. A knickerbocker is a New Yorker whose **ancestors** came from Holland in the 1600s. The team name is almost always shortened to Knicks.

Dave DeBusschere (22) was one of the Knicks who helped the team win two NBA titles in the 1970s.

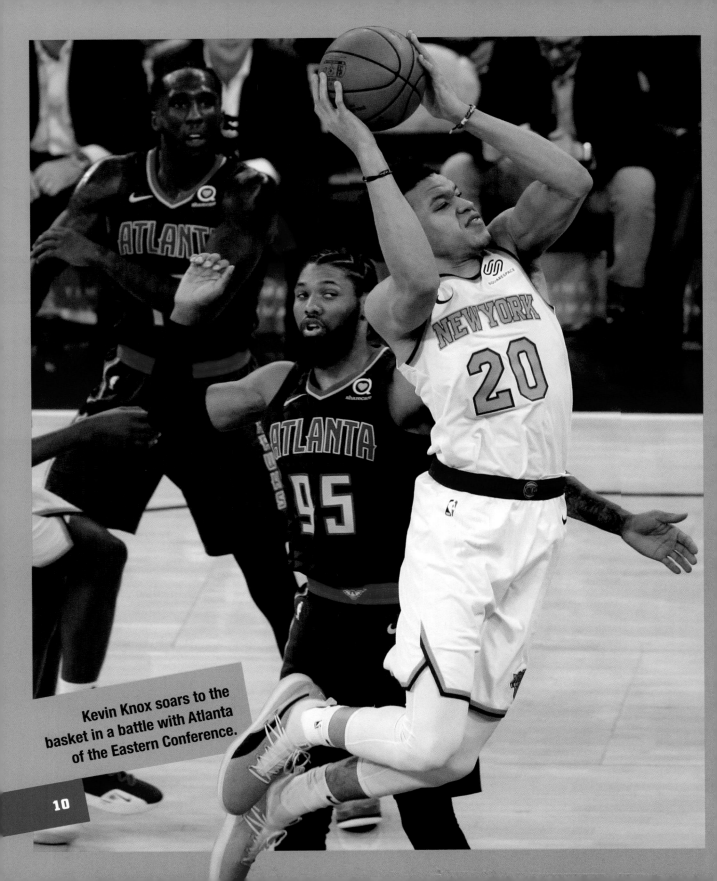

Kevin Knox soars to the basket in a battle with Atlanta of the Eastern Conference.

The Knicks play 82 games each season. They play 41 games at home and 41 on the road. They play four games against the other Atlantic Division teams. The Knicks also play 36 games against other Eastern Conference teams. Finally, they play each of the teams in the Western Conference twice. The winners of the Western and Eastern Conference play each other in the NBA Finals in June.

# WHERE THEY PLAY

The Knicks play their home games at Madison Square Garden. It is sometimes called MSG. It is one of the most famous **arenas** in the world. MSG hosts basketball games, hockey games, boxing matches, music concerts, and much more. There have been four different MSGs. The Knicks have played in the current MSG since 1968.

Madison Square Garden is sometimes called "the most famous arena in sports."

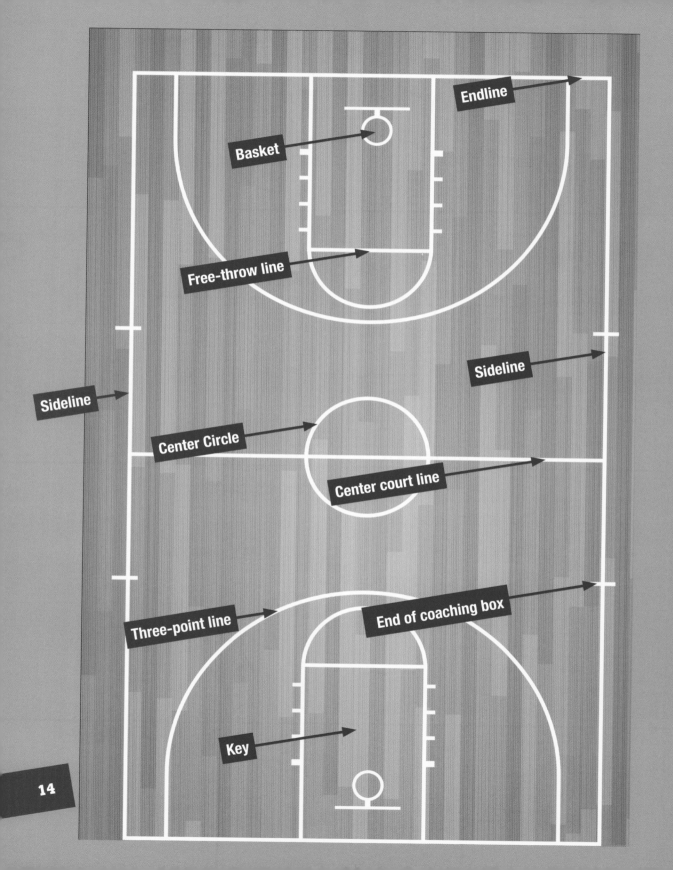

Endline

Basket

Free-throw line

Sideline

Sideline

Center Circle

Center court line

Three-point line

End of coaching box

Key

# THE BASKETBALL COURT

**A**n NBA court is 94 feet long and 50 feet wide (28.6 m by 15.24 m). Nearly all the courts are made from hard maple wood. Rubber mats under the wood help make the floor springy. Each team paints the court with its logo and colors. Lines on the court show the players where to take shots. The diagram on the left shows the important parts of the NBA court.

The Knicks' locker room in Madison Square Garden is round. This is unusual for the NBA. Also, no player walks on the team logo at the center of the room.

# GOOD TIMES

The Knicks were one of the best teams in the NBA's early years. They made the Finals three seasons in a row in the 1950s. They did not win a title until 1970, though. Then they won again in 1973. Star center Patrick Ewing joined the team in 1986. The Knicks soon started a streak of 14 seasons in a row in the playoffs.

Willis Reed leads his team to the locker room with a smile. The Knicks just won the 1973 NBA title!

Not even All-Star Carmelo Anthony could handle this play for the Knicks in their tough 2015 season.

18

# TOUGH TIMES

The Knicks lost a lot of games in 1985. They went 24–58. However, they won the **lottery** for the top pick in that year's draft. It brought Patrick Ewing to the team. His last season with the Knicks was in 2000. The team hit a dry spell soon after. The bottom came in 2015. They won only 17 games. It was their worst season ever.

# ALL THE RIGHT MOVES

**J**amal Crawford played for the Knicks from 2005 to 2009. He had a great **crossover** move. It even got its own name. It was called the "Shake and Bake." Basketball players use the crossover move while dribbling. It lets them quickly run past defenders. Current Knicks guard Dennis Smith often uses the move, too.

NBA players have to learn to dribble well with both hands. They practice many hours a day!

After making a crossover, Jamal Crawford heads to the hoop.

Smooth and speedy Walt Frazier had a Hall of Fame career with the Knicks.

**B**ill Bradley was a Hall of Fame forward for the Knicks. He was a star after basketball, too. He became a United States senator. Center Willis Reed is best known for hobbling off the bench in the playoffs in 1970. He inspired the Knicks to a title-clinching win. Walt Frazier and Earl Monroe were All-Star guards with cool nicknames. Frazier was "Clyde." Monroe was "Earl the Pearl."

The Knicks have high hopes for young forward Kevin Knox. They picked him in the first round of the 2018 NBA Draft. Knox was only 19 when he made his **debut**. He has become a solid all-around NBA player. Point guard Dennis Smith runs the offense. His passing fuels the Knicks offense. Emmanuel Mudiay grew up in the Congo in Africa. Now he slams home baskets for the Knicks.

Dennis Smith joined the Knicks in 2018 and quickly became a key player.

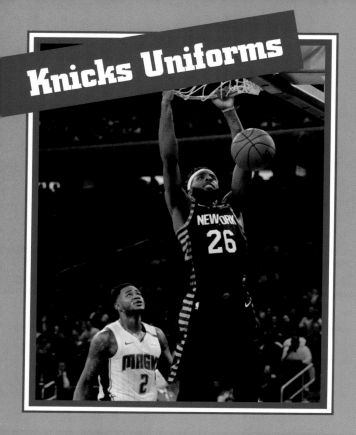

26

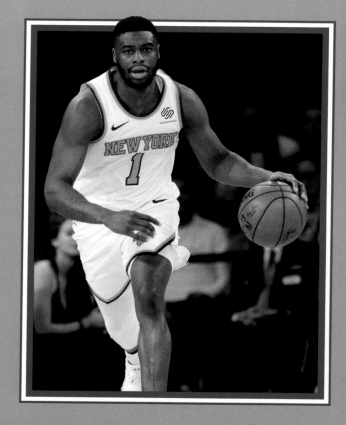

# WHAT
# THEY WEAR

**N**BA players wear a **tank top** jersey. Players wear team shorts. Each player can choose his own sneakers. Some players also wear knee pads or wrist guards.

Each NBA team has more than one jersey style. The pictures at left show some of the Knicks' jerseys.

The NBA basketball is 29.5 inches (75 cm) around. It is covered with leather. The leather has small bumps called pebbles.

The pebbles on a basketball help players grip it.

# TEAM STATS

H ere are some of the all-time career records for the New York Knicks. These stats are complete through all of the 2018–19 NBA regular season.

## ASSISTS PER GAME

| | |
|---|---|
| Mark Jackson | 8.0 |
| Micheal Ray Richardson | 7.1 |

## POINTS PER GAME

| | |
|---|---|
| Bob McAdoo | 26.7 |
| Bernard King | 26.5 |

## STEALS PER GAME

| | |
|---|---|
| Micheal Ray Richardson | 2.6 |
| Walt Frazier | 2.0 |

## REBOUNDS PER GAME

| | |
|---|---|
| Walt Bellamy | 13.3 |
| Willis Reed | 12.9 |

## THREE-POINT FIELD GOALS

| | |
|---|---|
| John Starks | 982 |
| Allan Houston | 921 |

## FREE-THROW PCT.

| | |
|---|---|
| Mike Glenn | .8862 |
| Kiki Vandeweghe | .8858 |

PATRICK EWING

## GAMES

| | |
|---|---|
| Patrick Ewing | 1,039 |
| Walt Frazier | 759 |

# GLOSSARY

**ancestors** *(ANN-cess-turs)* members of a family from earlier generations

**arenas** *(uh-REE-nuhz)* the buildings in which a basketball team plays its games

**crossover** *(KROSS-oh-ver)* a type of dribble in which the ball goes from one hand to the other

**debut** *(day-BYOO)* someone or something's first appearance

**drought** *(DROWT)* going without something for a period of time

**lottery** *(LAH-ter-ee)* a drawing whose outcome is determined by chance

**senator** *(SEH-nuh-tur)* an elected member of the US Senate

**tank top** *(TANK TOP)* a style of shirt that has straps over the shoulders and no sleeves

# FIND OUT MORE

## IN THE LIBRARY

*Big Book of Who: Basketball (Sports Illustrated Kids Big Books).* New York, NY: Sports Illustrated Kids, 2015.

Doeden, Matt. *The NBA Playoffs: In Pursuit of Basketball Glory.* Minneapolis, MN: Millbrook Press, 2019.

Whiting, Jim. *The New York Knicks (The NBA: A History of Hoops).* Mankato, MN: Creative Paperbacks, 2017.

## ON THE WEB

Visit our website for links about the New York Knicks:
**childsworld.com/links**

Note to Parents, Teachers, and Librarians: We routinely verify our Web links to make sure they are safe and active sites. So encourage your readers to check them out!

# INDEX